We Remember
THE BLACK BATTALION

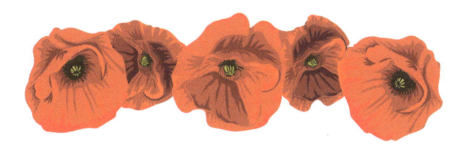

By Serena Virk
Illustrator Arnab Das

Dad

♥

Love you

Miss you

Acknowledgements

I appreciate and acknowledge the contribution of everyone whose assistance made this book possible to complete.

Many thanks to Rielle Simone Williams from the Black Cultural Centre for Nova Scotia, for her insights into the No. 2 Construction Battalion. Her helpful guidance and useful suggestions helped with the clarity and accuracy of the book.

I would also like to thank the Chatham-Kent Black Historical Society, Museum Windsor and Nova Scotia Archives for their contribution in providing historical pictures of the Black Battalion members. Pictures are vital for all of us to remember what happened in the past.

Lastly, I would like to thank my family for their encouragement, ideas and support through the whole process.

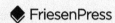 FriesenPress

One Printers Way
Altona, MB R0G 0B0
Canada

www.friesenpress.com

Copyright © 2022 by Serena Virk
First Edition — 2022

Illustrator - Arnab Das

Book cover - P6110 (courtesy of Museum Windsor)

All rights reserved.

No part of this publication may be reproduced in any form, or by any means, electronic or mechanical, including photocopying, recording, or any information browsing, storage, or retrieval system, without permission in writing from FriesenPress.

ISBN
978-1-03-915010-2 (Hardcover)
978-1-03-915009-6 (Paperback)
978-1-03-915011-9 (eBook)

1. JUVENILE NONFICTION, HISTORY, CANADA

Distributed to the trade by The Ingram Book Company

Men volunteered to fight during World War 1,

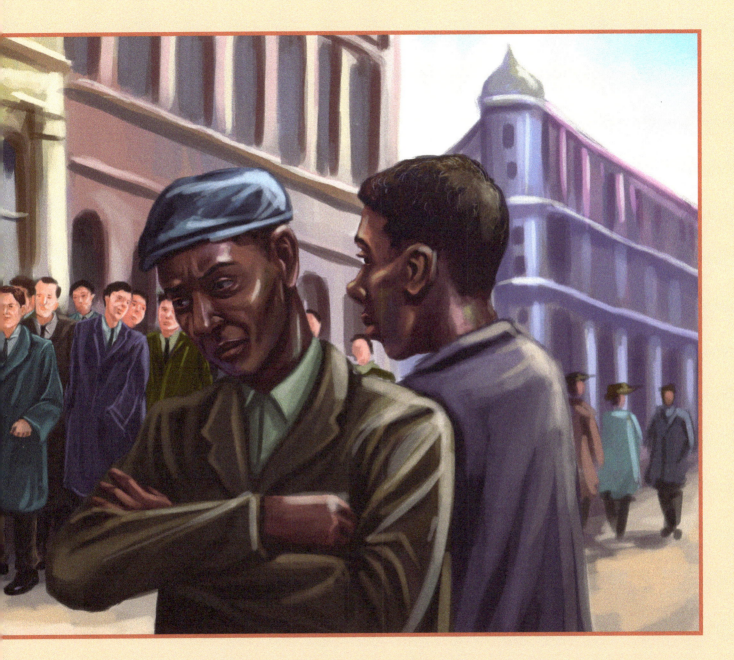

but not everyone was welcomed.

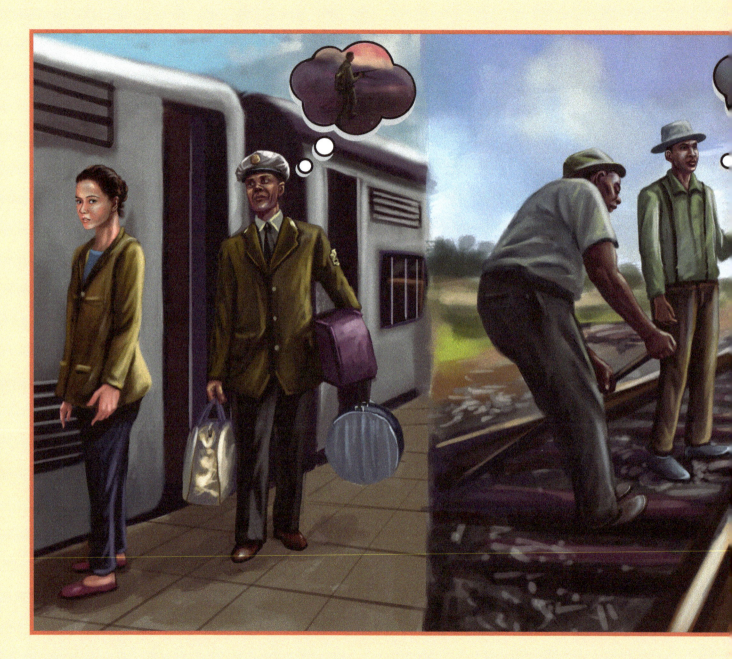

Men who wanted to help their country, their nation, their Canada;

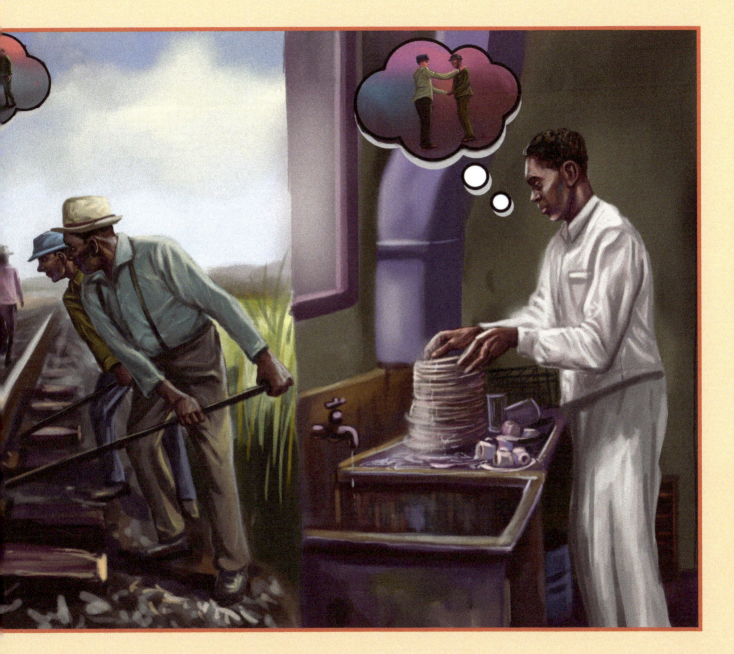
though they were not allowed.

Simply because of the colour of their skin.

Simply because they were Black.

The No. 2 Construction Black Battalion was created

specifically for Black men.

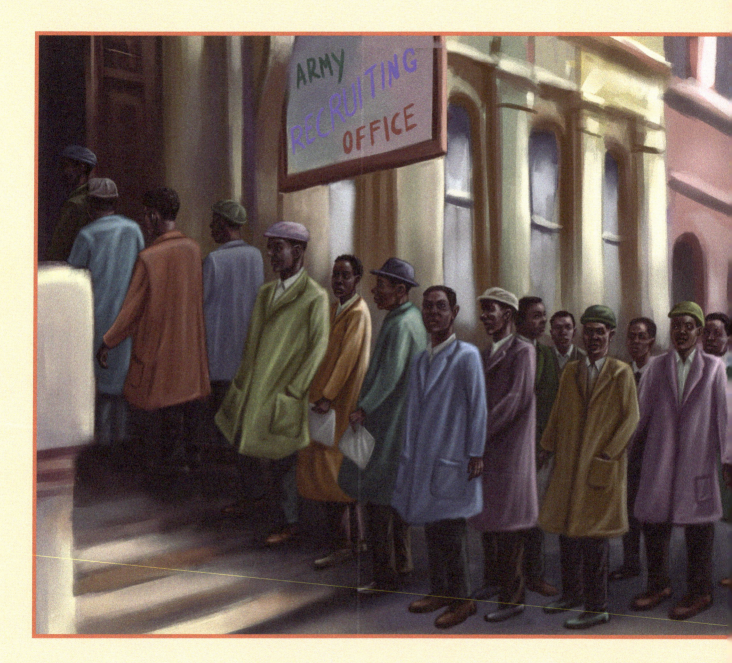

News of the Black Battalion spread.

Six hundred five men joined.

Men from Canada, the USA, and the British West Indies,

men ready to fight in the quarrel.

They were not given the same rights as others;

they faced racism and discrimination.

They were ready for battle; they were soldiers.

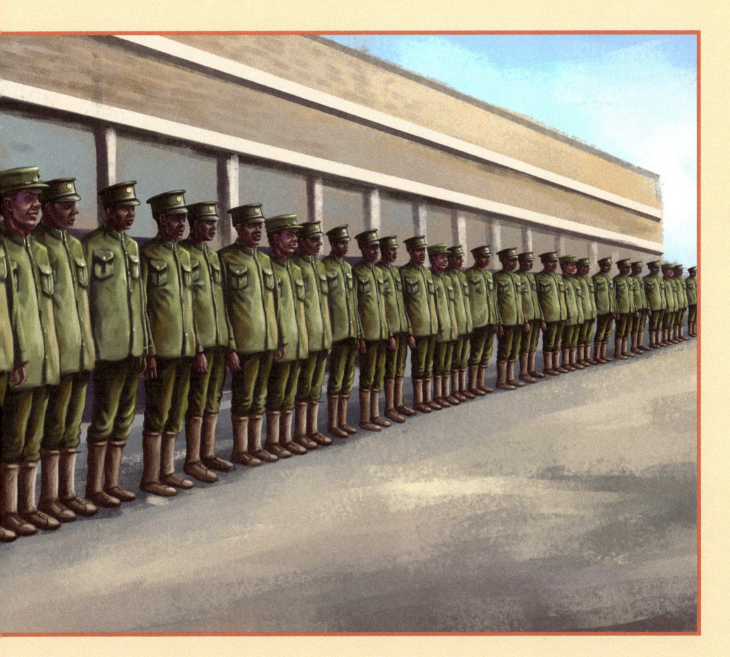

They were men who were not allowed to fight.

Their job was to cut lumber,

to rebuild the roads and railway tracks,

to lay down barbed wire,

to dig and build trenches,

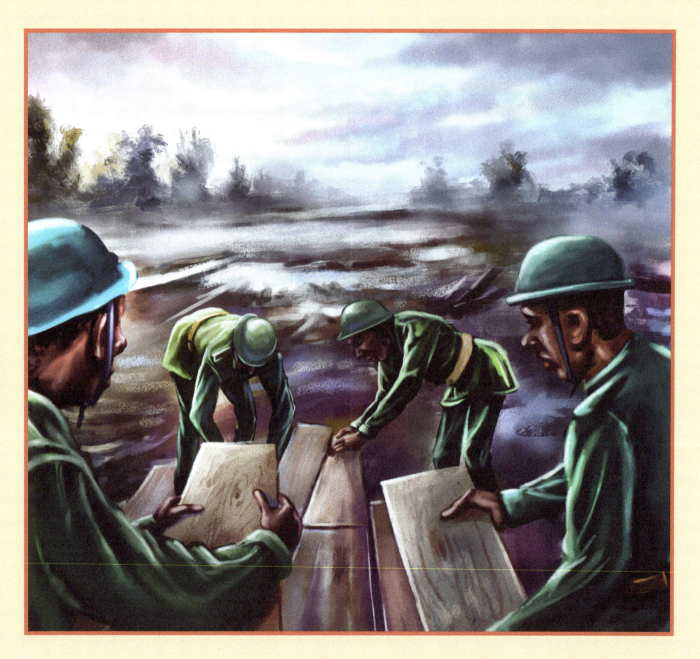

to make wooden walkways through the mud of the battlefield,

and to help the wounded move back.

They were given shovels,

not rifles.

They were given pickaxes,

not ammunition.

They were not fighting side-by-side with their allies as equals,

they were segregated.

They were the same as others,

but were never seen the same.

They served their country with pride and courage,

and we remember their names.

We Remember...

(No. 2 Construction Battalion, 1916; Nova Scotia
Archives, States Collection acc. no. 1981-337)

The Black Battalion

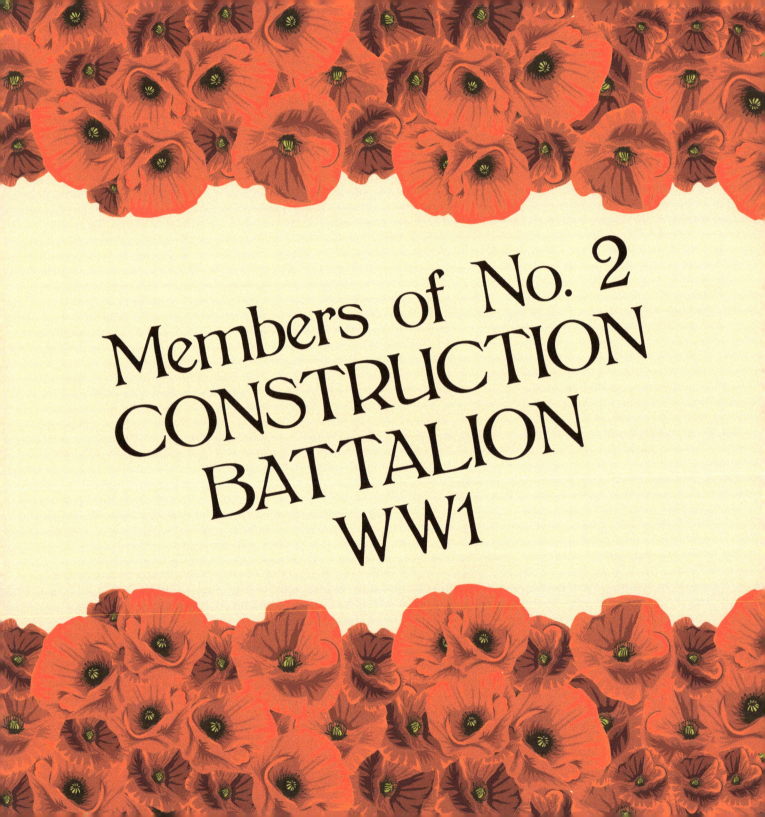

(courtesy of Chatham-Kent Black Historical Society)

Arthur Wright

(courtesy of Chatham-Kent Black Historical Society)

Cornellius Wright

(courtesy of Chatham-Kent Black Historical Society)

Jack Morris, Enoch Robbins, Fred Robinson and Hawkins

(courtesy of Chatham-Kent Black Historical Society)

William Thomas Jackson, Peter Browning, Ellery Jackson

P6110 (courtesy of Museum Windsor)

Reflection Questions

1. After reading the story, what do you think or wonder?

2. What part of the story spoke to you?

3. Stories create images with their words and express emotions. Which words or sentences from the story stood out for you? Which part made you think?

Glossary

Discrimination: Discrimination is the unfair treatment of one particular person or group of people. Discrimination based on race is called racism.

> "discrimination." kids.britannica.com. 2021.
> https://kids.britannica.com/kids/article/discrimination/399429 (20 May 2021).

Racism: Racism is when people are treated unfairly because of their skin colour or background. Racism is a form of discrimination that causes great harm to people.

> "racism." kids.britannica.com. 2021.
> https://kids.britannica.com/kids/article/racism/632495 (20 May 2021).

Segregated: Segregated means keeping people apart. In many cases, it is a form of discrimination and racism.

> "segregation." kids.britannica.com. 2021.
> https://kids.britannica.com/kids/article/segregation/632620 (20 May 2021).

CPSIA information can be obtained
at www.ICGtesting.com
Printed in the USA
BVHW020351200922
647447BV00002B/3